Mindful Meditation For Anxiety

HOW TO STOP ANXIETY

Learn To Overcome The Triggers Head On

MABEL WOODS

Table of Contents

Chapter 1:

Mindful Meditation For Anxiety

Practicing mindfulness meditation can be an effective way to deal with feelings of stress and anxiety, and it can also be used as a relaxation technique for panic disorder. When you first start meditating, you may be surprised at how difficult it is to sit still. Believe it or not, part of practicing mindfulness is realizing that sitting still can put your thoughts into a turbo drive. The key is not to judge the mind but to observe. Practice your sessions in minutes to get started. You can gradually increase the time by getting into a more regular habit. It is also important to meditate in a place where you are not distracted by others or distracted by people, pets, or phones. Remove shoes and heavy jewelry or restrictive clothing. The goal is to meditate in a space that is as quiet and comfortable as possible. Once you've decided on a time and place, start laying the groundwork for your meditation practice in these four steps:

Many people sit cross-legged on the floor with high spines. It is recommended that you sit with your legs straight, sit upright in a chair, or lie on your back. Find a position where you are comfortable enough not to be distracted but not unconscious or comfortable enough to fall asleep. You can change your place at any time if you experience discomfort or muscle cramps.

When you feel comfortable in a quiet place, focus on yourself. Close your eyes and start breathing. Notice your breathing patterns. But don't try to change it. It will help you recognize the present moment. When you notice that your mind is wandering, pay attention to your breathing. Breathe deeply to maintain relaxation while observing the natural rhythm of breathing.

Meditating at first may increase anxiety or self-esteem. Am I doing it right? What should I do? Instead of suppressing this internal conversation, recognize it and wait for it to pass. It will help you learn to sit down with unpleasant thoughts and not react. Over time, you may feel less anxious and feel more inner peace.

When you feel that your meditation is over or have reached your desired time, open your eyes. Do a few gentle stretches to break free from reflection gradually. Take some time to think about your practice. It can be challenging to keep track of time while meditating. If you're worried about running out of time, try using a quiet alarm or timer. This allows you to divert your attention from the watch and return to your workout.

Once you've got the basics down, you'll notice a significant decrease in previous signs of anxiety, such as reflection on past events or insomnia. But, as with all other methods, this may take some practice. Experiment with your exercises to find what works best for you. Mindfulness meditation can be done at any time of the day. Meditation after waking up may help reduce morning anxiety. Or you may find that evening meditation can help you get a good night's sleep. Try different times of the day to determine what works best for you.

Starting a meditation practice can be challenging, from finding a time and place on a busy schedule to facing frightening, judgmental thoughts that can cause anxiety. Consistently - even for a few minutes a day - you can find a practice that works for you, and you will see your anxiety and panic symptoms decrease.

Like any other meditation, mindfulness can be incorporated into daily activities. The informal practice works almost everywhere. Bring a mindful breath to your life by spending minutes at home, at work, at the hospital, bus stop, or even waiting in line. You can also make it a habit to practice mindful breathing right after waking up, during your morning break, during lunch, during the day, at night, or just before going to bed. After practicing mindful breathing during this time, you can try using it when you're a little anxious to help calm your body's panic attacks.

Chapter 2:

A Guided Journal For Anxiety

Anxiety Is The Silent Killer

Anxiety is a state of worry when you are unsure about the next step. Very few people know how to handle anxiety when they face it. Instead, they bury their heads in the sand and hope that things will eventually work themselves out.

What remains unclear are the disastrous results of actions resulting from anxiety. Healthy relationships have collapsed when partners succumbed to anxiety, job opportunities have been lost, and once-in-a-lifetime chances have slipped from our hands because we were unable to contain the anxiety that was building in us.

We will lose count of the much that anxiety has cost us. Sometimes, it has been misconstrued as a "normal" feeling and nothing is done to tame it. That is the moment the rain starts beating us. Nothing much can be done when we realize the damage anxiety has done in our lives.

Here is a guided journal for anxiety:

Take A Step Back

Sometimes we are anxious because we do not understand what we are into. We get nervous about new experiences and do not know how to proceed from there. Our judgment is often clouded when we are in unfamiliar territories. The fear of not being right builds anxiety in us and we want to please everybody. What a herculean task!

Take a step back to get the bigger picture. This will bring clarity because you can look at all variables at once and weigh them, one after another. Moving back gives you a sense of power and control when you realize it was not that difficult in the first place. You will be more comfortable in an environment you can manipulate.

Anxiety results from the fear of the unknown. When you withdraw a little from a situation, you can comfortably evaluate it because nobody will judge you.

Take Off Your Mind from The Subject Matter

This is an evasion strategy. You are not always required to face your fears immediately. It is okay to withdraw your attention when you are anxious about something or an unprecedented condition. You will live to tackle it another day. Do not pressure yourself to act within a deadline. The timeframes you confine yourself within will haunt you especially when you feel inadequate for what is ahead of you.

Put your mind on things that bring you solace and calm to fight the anxiety. You understand yourself better than anyone does and you are best placed to make this decision. Think about your dream car – Rolls-Royce, Ferrari, Porsche, Chevrolet, or any other that fascinates you. Relaxing thoughts will calm you down and kick away anxiety.

Our comfort zones give us confidence because we can handle ourselves better in them. Anxiety cannot win the battle when we are in them.

Do Not Think Of Any Consequences – There Are None

There are no consequences of acting right. What gives anxiety room to thrive is the fear of consequences that will befall us if we do not act expectedly. Deny anxiety the pleasure of tormenting you by not accepting liability for doing the right thing.

Even in situations that present a dilemma, choose to do the right thing over the popular choice. Populism is not always right, and its consequences are unavoidable. They will finally come to haunt you. To be safe, make the right choice whose consequences are positive and will bring you honor.

Regardless of how quickly you will want to work on your anxiety and make a popular choice, its results are indelible. Purpose to cure anxiety through the right channel with positive consequences.

Consult Widely

Consultations are the preserve of the wise. Only the wise accept that they do not have a monopoly of ideas. They seek the opinions of other people who could have had a similar experience. When you find yourself in a compromising situation, remember that you are not the first person to experience the same. Someone else has been there and they made it.

Anxiety grows in ignorance. You get nervous because you do not know how to handle the challenge your way. Seek the advice of experienced people and they will guide you on how to navigate unchartered territories.

In conclusion, anyone could be anxious. What makes the difference is how different people handle it. Some turn it into an opportunity for growth while others allow it to kill their dreams. Make the right choice.

Chapter 3:

Mindfulness Over Anxiety

Anxiety The Thief!

You may not realize it until the moment it steals your joy. Anxiety is the modern-day thief that deprives people of their joy. It camouflages behind various excuses but finally reveals its true colors. It is just a matter of time.

Anxiety instills worry for no good reason. All of a sudden you start to think 'what if things go wrong' when nothing has happened yet. This mentality will lie that you are planning ahead while the reality is that you are overstretching your ability. There is only so much that you can control.

Cheat Anxiety Today!

When you are anxious about something, your body will naturally respond to your fears. You tend to breathe a little faster than the normal rate, some people will sweat in their palms, and you will be absent-minded. Your mind will wander to how you can rescue yourself from the fix you find yourself in.

You can overcome anxiety in two ways: the short way and the long durable one.

The shorter way is regulating your basal metabolic rate. Here is what you should do whenever you are anxious. Inhale and exhale slowly paying attention to only the flow of air into and out of your lungs. Close your eyes as you do this.

Repeating this procedure will calm you down, your breathing rate will return to normal and you will regain your composure in a while.

While you may have beaten anxiety at the moment, you need a durable solution for it.

Mindfulness It Is!

Mindfulness is prioritizing logic over emotions no matter how strong they may be. Whenever you are anxious, tell yourself "Mindfulness over anxiety."

It happens in several ways but here are proven ways to overcome anxiety:

1. Take Caution

Most people throw caution to the wind about other matters except their cause for anxiety.

This is a dangerous trend because instead of curing anxiety, it will shift it elsewhere. Solving one problem only to create another is a cycle you will not want to be in.

Since anxiety is caused by worry, when you are careful about what you do there will be no cause for worry because you will ensure what is in your control unfolds just fine. Tie any loose ends to your plans to reduce risk and you will not have to worry about mishaps.

2. Build Healthy Relationships

You are probably anxious about somebody else's reaction because the both of you have not bonded well. This gives room to insecurities – a very unhealthy component of relationships.

It is difficult to be anxious about people that do not matter. The people you love and care for the most are the ones responsible for your anxiety.

Endeavor to build healthy relationships with them so that you can be confident of expressing yourself to them on anything, whether good or bad.

Healthy relationships are our refuge even during anxious moments and they should not be the very cause of our trouble.

3. Nourishing Your Mind

You should constantly feed your mind with the right things. Failure to do this, our fears take root and it becomes difficult to remove them.

Read widely and fill your mind with knowledge. Expand your expertise in science, astronomy, and whatever interests you. This will give no room for fear and anxiety to thrive.

Moreover, you can come up with solutions to what causes anxiety if you have the right skills. We are anxious when we are helpless. Having the knowledge to 'rescue' ourselves from such moments is good because we will always be in charge.

4. Planning To Reduce Risk

Uncertainty is what causes anxiety. The future is a gamble and not everything is guaranteed. When you plan, you will feel more secure and so will the people you are with. There will be surety about many things that would have otherwise cost you sleepless nights.

Mindfulness over anxiety includes these four and many other steps to curb anxiety before it even sprouts. You shall eventually emerge victoriously.

Chapter 4:

Meditation The Key To Happiness

Have you ever wondered why people who meditate tend to be the happiest, most grateful and satisfied people on earth? And have you ever wondered why the rest of us always seem to be unhappy about everything that is going on with our lives even though we are incredibly fortunate to be alive?

Many of us have a roof over our heads, smartphones that keeps us connected all the time, friends and family that surround us, but yet we still can't explain why we aren't at peace inside.

We get bogged down by traffic, people around us who seem to rub us the wrong way, and the countless other things that seem to bring us closer and closer to anguish.

Another problem that many of us have to deal with right now is stress. we have deadlines, colleagues, bosses, and paperwork that bring us overwhelm on a daily basis that we find ourselves off balance and in search of our breath.

I want to introduce you to the powerful tool called meditation, and why it is crucial that you employ it in your lives to reduce stress and anxiety and to live a more mindful life starting today.

When we meditate, even to a short 5-10min guided meditation practice that can be found on YouTube or even right here on this channel, we bring our awareness to the present moment. And when we breathe and focus on the breath, we allow time for ourselves to be grounded and centered. When thoughts enter our mind, we simply acknowledge them and let them drift on by. This conscious practice of being fully present and deep breathing allows our bodies to relax and destress. And we are much more focused on what we need to do and how we can get to our goals faster.

Through meditation, one can change and rewire our brain to stop thinking of the past and future but to focus on the here and now. With intention, meditation can also help you get what you needed to done faster.

Through my own meditation practice, i have found that it made every day of my life much more purposeful and grounded. Before, i always found myself drifting throughout the day, wasting time, procrastinating, and feeling guilty for not taking action. But with a simple 10min guided meditation practice, i was able to refocus my attention and get my day going as it should without feeling sorry that i had wasted my morning not getting anything done.

Meditation takes time to develop, like a muscle, consistency is the key to success. By devoting 10mins each day to meditation, you are telling yourself that this is the time for yourself, time to reframe all the negative thoughts, to be grateful for your existence, to not dwell on the past, and to focus on the things and people that matter in life. Your body will essentially be "tricked" into automatically feeling abundance, happiness, and joy. The more you do it, the more powerful this technique becomes.

I challenge each and every one of you to try out meditation for yourself, even if I am only able to get through to one person, i am sure you will experience the rich and rewarding experience that meditation can do for you today.

Chapter 5:

Meditate to Rewire Your Brain for Happiness

Suppose you've ever read the book Bridge to Terabithia (or seen the movie). In that case, you are familiar with Terabithia – an imaginary world that the main characters, Jesse and Leslie, create as a haven. It is somewhere they can go to be free from the cares and worries of the world.

Meditation has given me a Terabithia. I have created a clearing of calm and tranquility that I can enter into within seconds whenever I feel the need. I have a refuge no matter where I am or what I am doing. The worries of the world no longer threaten me. Except this mental place isn't imaginary, and it isn't populated with trolls and wild creatures – it is as real as the world we live in.

Since starting my meditation habit, my brain has been rewired for happiness, peace, and success. Here are just a few of the benefits:

I rarely become angry.

I find happiness in unexpected places.

I form deeper relationships and build friendships more easily.

However, by far, the largest benefit is that a deep, serene calm and peace is slowly permeating into every area of my life. At first, meditating felt unusual – like I was stepping out of normal life and doing something that most people find strange. I soon realized, however, that this wasn't true – millions of people meditate, and many successful people attribute part of their success to meditation.

Oprah Winfrey, Hugh Jackman, Richard Branson, Paul McCartney, Angelina Jolie... Any of these names sound familiar? All of these are famous meditators.

This list alone is powerful, but maybe you need a little more convincing that meditation is something you should try.

Michael Jordan, Kobe Bryant, Misty-May Trainor, and Derek Jeter are just a few successful athletes who rely on meditation to get them in the zone.

Rupert Murdoch, Russell Simons, and Arianna Huffington all practice meditation.

Arnold Schwarzenegger and Eva Mendez are just a couple more celebrities that make meditation a daily habit.

Meditation Reduces Stress

Are you feeling the weight of the world on your shoulders? Meditation is incredibly effective at reducing stress and anxiety. One study found that mindfulness and zen-type meditations significantly reduce stress when practiced over a period of three months. Another study revealed that meditation reduces the density of brain tissue associated with anxiety and worrying. If you want your stress levels to plummet, meditation may be the answer.

Chapter 6:

Mindfulness For Depression

10 minutes a day is all it takes to gain better control of your thoughts and strengthen your ability to handle strong emotions. A fact is: you only get one mind. Mindfulness will help you take good care of it.

The benefits of using mindfulness for depression are extensive. Practicing mindfulness meditation for 10 minutes a day can change the structure of your brain and prevent you from falling back into depression after getting well. Better yet, your mindfulness practice won't produce the uncomfortable side effects that usually come with antidepressant medication.

Are you a fan of learning by doing? If so, do the following exercise before we go on exploring the five simple steps of mindfulness for depression:

- Focus on your breathing for about 10 seconds

- Pay attention to the sensations in your body when you breathe in and out

- Without judging if they're good or bad, try to describe the sensations to yourself (e.g. you may feel expanding and contracting, chest and stomach moving, your heartbeat, tightness, relaxation…).

Congratulations! You just completed a 10-second mindfulness practice. It doesn't have to be more complicated than that. When practicing mindfulness for depression, there is no need for incense, crossed legs or chanting. It's easiest to start your mindfulness practice with recorded meditation exercises (find one below), but mindfulness can also be practiced in every-day situations, for example when taking a walk or a shower. Mindfulness is paying attention to the present moment without judging what you find. This can be achieved by simply closing your eyes and notice what's going on inside you. Actually, you don't even need to close your eyes. Some mindfulness practitioners prefer to stare into a flame or at the floor when meditating. Also, you can practice mindfulness simply by noticing the things around you, such as the colour of the sky, the smell of your coffee or the sensation of wind on your face. This means that mindfulness basically is to notice what happens, whatever that is. And you do this in five simple steps:

1. Direct your focus to the present moment (for example by noticing sounds, smells, your breathing or the emotions in your body).

2. Try not to judge what you find.

3. Get distracted by thoughts (this is part of the deal and simply how the human mind works).

4. When you get distracted (because you will), kindly bring back your focus to the present moment.

5. Repeat step 1-4 over and over again.

Simply put, mindfulness is a way to practice paying attention. Are you easily distracted by thoughts? Most people are. And when going through depression, those thoughts tend to become extra negative and persistent. Using mindfulness for depression will help you become more aware of your usual automatic thought processes and you'll discover that it's possible to actually choose what to pay attention to.

Depression makes us pay special attention to negative experiences, thoughts and feelings. And sometimes a depressed mind will automatically turn neutral happenings into negative ones. By practicing mindfulness we train the brain to give us a more realistic view of ourselves and others. We take control of our minds, instead of letting the autopilot decide what to focus on.

Starting a new mindfulness practice can be a difficult task if you're unprepared for some of the common problems that beginner meditators usually experience. In this section, we'll go through two common difficulties with using mindfulness for depression: absent-mindedness and high performance.

Absent-mindedness. A common mistake that beginner mindfulness practitioners often make is to think of thoughts as disturbing or distracting, when they're actually an essential part of mindfulness practice. Did you notice thoughts popping into your head during the meditation exercise above? Then, congratulations! Mindfulness meditation is to constantly note distracting thoughts and bring back your focus. Over and over again. Yes, it can be frustrating, but also great exercise for your brain. Every time you bring back your focus it's like you're doing a bicep curl for your mind. When meditating, you will probably have negative thoughts such as "this is stupid"; "I'm too restless"; "this will never work". All such thoughts give you the opportunity to redirect your attention and exercise your brain. And if they are really crappy thoughts, try to give them a name, such as "the Critic", "the Judge", "Mrs Panic" or something else. Naming these intrusive characters in your head can help getting some distance from them.

In conclusion, mindfulness is paying attention to the present moment without judging what you find. Practicing this skill has proven to be very beneficial for the brain and for reducing the risk of depression.

Chapter 7:

10 Ways To Stop Anxiety

Everyone experiences some anxious moments in their busy lives. Anxiety is, in fact, scientifically proven as the most common mental health issue. It may not be a cause for concern on the one hand, but it may be detrimental to you, on the other hand. Anxiety interferes with your ability to make decisions, hence preventing you from having a normal life.

Being anxious and dealing with it is never easy. The ability to handle anxiety is a long-term process that doesn't happen spontaneously. However, there are various techniques that have been proven effective when incorporated into your daily routine. When anxiety is a little over the top, consider the following management strategies.

Here are 10 ways to stop anxiety.

1. Meditation

Meditation is proven to be an excellent way of reducing anxiety and enhancing your intuition, lowering blood pressure, and increasing your focus. Meditating calms anxious thoughts and reduces the body's reaction to such unpleasant feelings. Take a break and practice a meditation ritual; you can go for a jog, do yoga, take deep breaths, or do other relaxation techniques. Relaxing or calming your body is proven to develop your mind-set, or the "inner game," essential for your mental health.

2. Treat the Underlying Cause of Stress

In addition to temporarily alleviating anxiety symptoms, consider looking into the root causes. Create a checklist of what you're in control of and those you can't. Then, put your focus on addressing issues you can control. For instance, if your debts keep you awake at night, devise a strategy to solve them. Turn your anxious thoughts into productive action whenever possible.

3. Understand Your Fear

Merely trying to suppress your anxious thoughts may worsen your situation. Persuading yourself not to think about it is likely to rebound. The widely publicized "white bear experiment" in 1987 highlighted this perplexing impact where the respondents admitted to seeing more 'white bears.' Just accept that you are anxious, and that your extraneous thoughts will eventually go away.

4. Schedule Time for Your Feelings

Have you had a great deal of smoldering embers to extinguish? Consider setting time for the burning thoughts. Yes, it will appear to be illogical. Start by adding 'thinking time to your to-do list. Transitioning simply reacting to whatever comes your way to strategizing for your prospective future lessens your day-to-day fires and enables you to optimize what is pertinent.

5. Redefine Your Unreal Beliefs

Anxiety can lead to catastrophic predictions. Picturing your entire future being ruined by one unfortunate mistake or that one bad grade will leave you restless and will eventually fuel anxiety. Replace exaggeratedly negative statements with more realistic ones. When you find yourself imagining the worst-case scenario about a situation, constantly remind yourself that even if you mess up, it won't be the end.

6. Switch It Up

If you can't get your mind off from worrying, and if the situation is beyond your control, engage your body with something new. You can take a walk or clean your closet-whatever it takes to keep your mind occupied. Focusing your attention somewhere else, even for a few minutes, can help reduce your stress and pave a way for a much needed break your mind may need.

7. Start a Gratitude Journey

Do it every night; it works and its simple. Learn to appreciate the little things in your life. You can also keep a journal to write about your worrying moments and the steps you can take to overcome them.

8. Talk to Someone

Getting together with family and friends, even strangers at Starbucks, and talking about how you're feeling can be beneficial. If opening up is hard for you, consider other avenues like jotting it down or other online platforms.

9. Find A Quiet Space

Sights and sounds can frequently amplify a panic attack. Find a peaceful place to vent to whenever you feel anxious. Venting in a quiet place allows you to create a safer place for your mind, making it easier to practice mindfulness and other coping strategies.

10. Stay Away From Alcohol

Because alcohol is a natural sedative, it often takes the edge off first. However, research indicates a link between anxiety and alcohol consumption, with coexisting anxiety disorders and alcohol use disorder (AUD). Excessive consumption of alcohol interferes with your serotine levels which is also responsible for your mental health. Such imbalances often stimulate symptoms of anxiety in your body.

Conclusion

Anxiety is not a cause for alarm in most cases, but if left untreated, it can develop into a disorder that has a negative impact on your mental health. Consider the above anxiety management techniques whenever you feel anxious. And also, remember to seek professional help when needed.

Chapter 8:

Rid Yourself of Anxiety

What is it like living with an unknown fear, dread, restlessness, and nervousness? Seems odd and inappropriate. However, many of us are familiar with and face such emotions almost every day or occasionally. Your bad experiences, any loss you suffered, and traumas in past, triggers those anxious emotions.

Stressing over ordinary things like work, school, finances, and relationships is the most common cause of anxiety for most of us. Whenever you take on too much stress and pressure about something, you become more anxious. The more anxious you are, the more depressed and stressed you become about little things.

Sometimes this anxiety puts you in an embarrassing situation. You react weirdly when you have intense stress about little things.

Exaggerating things, pessimistic thinking, and overthinking play a vital role in anxiety and simply leads to depression and psychological distress. You become unable to concentrate, your thoughts become clouded and leave you with no direction. While we all experience normal anxiety during stressful situations, some people suffer from anxiety disorders and worry about minor things constantly and unnecessarily.

An average amount of anxiety can sometimes be beneficial. It can improve concentration and learning. In addition, it causes us to get anxious when we have an important task to complete or exams at school to prepare for. The stress of these things keeps you focused and alert. Fortunately, once the task is finished, this anxiety abates. But if this anxiety extends for a long period, it can affect your ability to learn and concentrate. In this situation, the brain shuts down so it cannot process, making the task more difficult.

It isn't worth it to try to achieve anything in life while you're stressed out. To succeed in life, you'll need to let go of this stress. So, what should you do to rid yourself of anxiety? Keep in mind that it is all in our heads. We control our emotions, thoughts, and feelings. As humans, we have all the power to control our lives. We just need to realize it.

Take charge of your life and make quick decisions. Don't spend hours thinking about little things like what to eat today? Or what to wear? As we strive for perfection in everything, we not only exhaust our time, but also limit our ability to make decisions, and sometimes, we even end up doing nothing, which is how we develop anxiety.

High standards and unrealistic expectations can also cause anxiety. And when you cannot reach that standard or accomplish it, you feel demotivated and think you are not able to achieve anything in life. That's where you start stressing. It causes a fear inside you, that always keeps you from the beginning, and you put things off for tomorrow; tomorrow that never comes. Don't try to accomplish everything at once. Take small steps and don't run over perfection. You don't need to wait for the perfect time, if you have the skills, just go for it now, without worrying whether it's good or bad, just go for it. It makes things easier for you if you want to accomplish something.

Living a risk-taking lifestyle gives you a sense of empowerment. This sense of freedom and courage replaces your anxiety, and you feel delighted doing everything. Take a chance on yourself and don't think too much. Trust yourself and believe in your abilities. With the right motivation and an optimistic outlook, you can accomplish anything in life.

Chapter 9:

Stop Dwelling on Things

It's 5 p.m., the deadline for an important work project is at 6, and all you can think about is the fight you had with the next-door neighbor this morning. You're dwelling. "It's natural to look inward," but while most people pull out when they've done it enough, an overthinker will stay in the loop."

Ruminating regularly often leads to depression. So, if you're prone to obsessing (and you know who you are), try these tactics to head off the next full-tilt mental spin cycle...

1.Distract Yourself

Go and exercise, scrub the bathtub spotless, put on music and dance, do whatever engrosses you, and do it for at least 10 minutes. That's the minimum time required to break a cycle of thoughts.

2. Make a Date to Dwell

Tell yourself you can obsess all you want from 6 to 7 p.m., but until then, you're banned. "By 6 p.m., you'll probably be able to think things through more clearly,"

3. 3 Minutes of Mindfulness

For one minute, eyes closed, acknowledge all the thoughts going through your mind. For the next minute, just focus on your breathing. Spend the last minute expanding your awareness from your breath to your entire body. "Paying attention in this way gives you the room to see the questions you're asking yourself with less urgency and to reconsider them from a different perspective,"

4.The Best and Worst Scenarios

Ask yourself...

"What's the worst that could happen?" and "How would I cope?" Visualizing yourself handling the most extreme outcome should alleviate some anxiety. Then consider the likelihood that the worst will occur.

Next, imagine the best possible outcome; by this point, you'll be in a more positive frame of mind and better able to assess the situation more realistically.

5. Call a Friend

Ask a friend or relative to be your point person when your thoughts start to speed out of control.

6. Is It Worth It?

If you find that your mind is fixated on a certain situation, ask yourself if the dwelling is worth your time.

'Ask yourself if looking over a certain situation will help you accept it, learn from it and find closure,' 'If the answer is no, you should make a conscious effort to shelve the issue and move on from it.'

7. Identify Your Anxiety Trigger

There may be a pattern in your worries, and this means you can help identify potential causes and use practice preventative measures.

'For many of us, rumination will occur after a trigger, so it is important to identify what it is,' 'For example, if you have to give a presentation at work and the last one you didn't go to plan, this can cause rumination and anxiety.

Chapter 10:

Choose Getting into Nature for Better Mood and Happiness

It's clear that hiking—and any physical activity—can reduce stress and anxiety. But, there's something about being in nature that may augment those impacts.

In one recent experiment conducted in Japan, participants were assigned to walk either in a forest or in an urban center (taking walks of equal length and difficulty) while having their heart rate variability, heart rate, and blood pressure measured. The participants also filled out questionnaires about their moods, stress levels, and other psychological measures.

Results showed that those who walked in forests had significantly lower heart rates and higher heart rate variability (indicating more relaxation and less stress) and reported better moods and less anxiety than those who walked in urban settings. The researchers concluded that there's something about being in nature that had a beneficial effect on stress reduction, above and beyond what exercise alone might have produced. In another study, researchers in Finland found that urban dwellers who strolled for as little as 20 minutes through an urban park or woodland reported significantly more stress relief than those who strolled in a city center.

The reasons for this effect are unclear, but scientists believe that we evolved to be more relaxed in natural spaces. In a now-classic laboratory experiment by Roger Ulrich of Texas A&M University and colleagues, participants who first viewed a stress-inducing movie, and were then exposed to color/sound videotapes depicting natural scenes, showed much quicker, more complete recovery from stress than those who'd been exposed to videos of urban settings.

These studies and others provide evidence that being in natural spaces— or even just looking out of a window onto a natural scene—somehow soothes us and relieves stress.Gregory Bratman of Stanford University has found evidence that nature may impact our mood in other ways, too.

In one 2015 study, he and his colleagues randomly assigned 60 participants to a 50-minute walk in either a natural setting (oak woodlands) or an urban setting (along a four-lane road). Before and after the walk, the participants were assessed on their emotional state and on cognitive measures, such as how well they could perform tasks requiring short-term memory. Results showed that those who walked in nature experienced less anxiety, rumination (focused attention on negative aspects of oneself), and negative affect, as well as more positive emotions, in comparison to the urban walkers. They also improved their performance on the memory tasks.

Chapter 11:

Feeling like You're Drowning in Stuff

By drowning, the first thing that comes to mind is drowning in A pool of water. Well, drowning in life is almost the same as drowning in water. Every time you drown, you need the help of A lifeguard or any other guy who can drag you out and save you. The same is the case with drowning in life; if you don't dig deep enough to come out of this phase, you need the help of an expert to help you feel better. When A person feels like drowning in stuff, most of the time, the reason is the hectic daily routine or the rush of emotions. When emotions start to build up to an extent where they become A burden, the affected person feels like being drowned in these emotions. This can further lead to stress and anxiety. If the feeling is due to work, it's because the person is working more than his brain and body can handle. This mostly happens to students who are working part-time to manage their expenses. The burden of study is already A big one, and once coupled to the workload, it becomes A mountain of A burden where the student doesn't get any time to relax.

There are many ways to overcome this feeling. The most effective one is to let your emotions out. Some councilors are there to listen to one's problems and find the perfect solution to them. If A person chooses to remain silent, he will be overwhelmed by these emotions/thoughts, and that is when these feelings turn into depression and anxiety. When depression kicks in, it's even harder to get back on track than it is when you are starting to have feelings of drowning. Now for students who are also working, they should find A way to relax every now and then. Relaxation is always A good solution to these problems. Taking some time out for yourself can prove to be healthy for both the body and the brain. The mind always produces positive thoughts when it is relaxed. Overburdening can lead to negative emotions and thoughts, which can lead to the feeling of being drowned.

Working out can be very helpful in times like these. It releases A hormone called endorphin which actually helps with stress and gives you joyful emotions. When the body is engaged in repetitive motions, the brain gets distracted from all burdens and only focuses on the tasks at hand, which in this case is exercise. So focusing only on one task helps the brain to relax and heal from all of the thoughts that were being processed before. After the workout, the person feels very light and positive because of this short relaxation of the brain.

Mental health professionals are there for those who are having A hard time dealing with the feeling of being drowned in stuff. One should never feel ashamed of talking to somebody about matters like these because it is for their good. Relying on medicines and other relaxants can lead to improper functioning of the brain. Still, practicing habits like taking counsel from professionals or simply giving time to oneself can prove to be very healthy as it helps the mind to focus better. Giving up isn't the option; surviving and eventually living the best life is.

Chapter 12:

Five Ways To Get Calm

The art of maintaining calm.

Calmness is an art that only a few people have mastered. Most people are erratic and easily unsettled by trivial matters. The state of calmness provides an optimum environment to work and meet your targets.

The modern world is full of people who seek solace in different deviations. They hope to find peace in a chaotic world. However, they only find temporary solutions to their problems and fail to secure calmness of mind and spirit.

Here are five ways to get calm:

1. Regulate Your Body's Metabolism

We may find ourselves in circumstances that make our bodies tense. We experience an adrenaline rush as a natural body response to tension. Our hearts beat faster, a pang of fear laced with anxiety sweeps through our minds, and we are unable to make sober decisions.

Calmness becomes elusive and we often act out of fear of the unknown. In such circumstances, our actions are not backed up by any rational thinking. How can we regain our composure and maintain calm? First, inhale sharply and exhale slowly to release the tension building up.

Repeat it until you manage to regulate your breathing. Inhaling and exhaling at regular intervals will bring calmness to replace the initial tension. Try to act as normal as possible and do not yield to any pressure to act, real or perceived.

2. Master Your Emotions

It takes great courage to master your emotions and reactions towards issues. A great man is capable of controlling his emotions and bringing calmness in chaotic situations. Calmness hardly prevails when emotions are high.

Emotions rid you of rationality and independent thinking. They control your actions and seek justification. Emotions are no respecter of persons. They have caused the downfall of many giants who did not let reason prevail.

Take charge of your emotions and do not yield to their temptations no matter how justifiable they may look. A master of emotions will bring calmness in their lives and they can settle things soberly.

3. Question Your Feelings

Your feelings are not always right. You could be biased and inclined to support certain things that disrupt calmness and are fodder to chaos. Subconscious feelings often present themselves as the truth and we believe unfounded theories that pose a danger to interpersonal relationships and by extension, societal harmony.

Calmness prevails where feelings and intuitions are evaluated before being acted upon. Learn to question your feelings and leave nothing to chance. For example, why do you hate the guard at the main gate or a political competitor? It is unfair to yourself not to understand the reason for the strong positions you take.

After questioning your feelings, you can re-evaluate hardline stances that you took which can jeopardize your calmness around people you consider hostile. You can manage to be calm and tolerant when you find no merit in your ill feelings towards something.

4. Question What You Stand to Benefit Or Lose

The chief question you should be able to answer is what you benefit from any chaos. There is disorderliness in the absence of calm, and it causes more harm than good. We are exposed to the risk of loss when the environment we live in is unstable. It is important to ensure it is calm for us to thrive in it and achieve our goals.

Many things run in the mind when one is provoked. What often skips the brain is whether or not the whole experience will be gainful. At this juncture, you think in retrospect concerning your life. Will a moment of anger make you lose what has taken long for you to build?

Such hard questions will eventually let calmness prevail. The fear of losing precious gains will bring calmness to maintain the status quo.

5. Selective Amnesia

Amnesia is a condition of forgetting things. The memory is compromised and one forgets everything that happened in their lives. It is undesirable but maybe you should consider it if you want to be calm. Selective amnesia is choosing to willfully ignore the ugly things that have happened.

When you realize that something irritates you, shut it out of your life to regain sanity. Calmness is an expensive gift that should be treasured. Nothing should deprive you of the right to enjoy the serenity of life.

Choose to look at the good side only of things. You can maintain calm by dwelling exclusively on it and refusing to give people the power to control you.

In conclusion, calmness is a trophy that should be on our shelves. These five ways to get calm are effective should we implement them correctly.

Chapter 13:

3 Ways To Calm The Emotional Storm Within You

When emotions are already intense, it's often hard to think about what you can do to help yourself, so the first thing you need to work on is getting re-regulated as quickly as possible. Here are some fast-acting skills that work by changing your body's chemistry; it will be most helpful if you first try these before you're in an emotional situation, so you know how to use them.

1. Do A Forward Bend

This is my favorite re-regulating skill. Bend over as though you're trying to touch your toes (it doesn't matter if you can actually touch your toes; you can also do this sitting down if you need to, by sticking your head between your knees). Take some slow, deep breaths, and hang out there for a little while (30 to 60 seconds if you can). Doing a forward bend actually activates our parasympathetic nervous system – our 'rest and digest' system – which helps us slow down and feel a little calmer. When you're ready to stand up again, just don't do it too quickly – you don't want to fall over.

2.   Focus On Your Exhale With 'Paced Breathing'

It might sound like a cliché but breathing truly is one of the best ways to get your emotions to a more manageable level. In particular, focus on making your exhale longer than your inhale – this also activates our parasympathetic nervous system, again helping us feel a little calmer and getting those emotions back to a more manageable level. When you inhale, count in your head to see how long your inhale is; as you exhale, count at the same pace, ensuring your exhale is at least a little bit longer than your inhale. For example, if you get to 4 when you inhale, make sure you exhale to at least 5. For a double whammy, do this breathing while doing your forward bend.

These re-regulating skills will help you to think a little more clearly for a few minutes, but your emotions will start to intensify once more if nothing else has changed in your environment – so the next steps are needed too.

3.   Increase Awareness Of Your Emotions

In order to manage emotions more effectively in the long run, you need to be more aware of your emotions and of all their components; and you need to learn to name your emotions accurately. This might sound strange – of course you know what you're feeling, right? But how do you know if what you've always called 'anger' is actually anger, and not anxiety? Most of us have never really given our emotions much thought, we just assume that what we think we feel is what we actually feel – just like we assume the colour we've always called 'blue' is actually blue; but how do we really know?

Sensitive people who have grown up in a pervasively invalidating environment often learn to ignore or not trust their emotional experiences, and try to avoid or escape those experiences, which contributes to difficulties naming emotions accurately. Indeed, anyone prone to emotion dysregulation can have trouble figuring out what they're feeling, and so walks around in an emotional 'fog'. When you're feeling 'upset', 'bad' or 'off', are you able to identify what emotion you're actually feeling? If you struggle with this, consider each of the following questions the next time you experience even a mild emotion:

- What was the prompting event or trigger for the feeling? What were you reacting to? (Don't judge whether your response was right or wrong, just be descriptive.)

- What were your thoughts about the situation? How did you interpret what was happening? Did you notice yourself judging, jumping to conclusions, or making assumptions?

- What did you notice in your body? For example, tension or tightness in certain areas? Changes in your breathing, your heart rate, your temperature?

- What was your body doing? Describe your body language, posture and facial expression.

- What urges were you noticing? Did you want to yell or throw things? Was the urge to not make eye contact, to avoid or escape a situation you were in?

- What were your actions? Did you act on any of the urges you noted above? Did you do something else instead?

Going through this exercise will help you increase your ability to name your emotions accurately. Once you've asked yourself the above questions, you could try asking yourself if your emotion fits into one of these four (almost rhyming) categories: mad, sad, glad, and afraid. These are terms I use with clients as a helpful starting point for distinguishing basic emotions, but gradually you can work on getting more specific; emotions lists can also be helpful.

Chapter 14:

4 Reasons Why You Feel Empty

The feeling of emptiness is stark in contrast to the emotions that a person is supposed to feel. It sits like a black hole in your chest, devoid of the substance that is supposed to be there. Here are some of the reasons why you feel empty

1. Absence Of Purpose

Many people struggle with finding a sense of purpose in this vast universe of limitless possibilities.

What do I do with my life? Does this mean anything? What should I be doing with myself?

The existential dread that comes with lacking purpose can fuel emptiness as it feels like we are missing something we are supposed to have. Some people try to fill the emptiness with their actions, like doing volunteer work or getting a job in a field that can help people.

Seeking purpose is an interesting matter because you may not be ready to find a particular purpose. And we don't mean that in an abstract, destiny kind of sense. Instead, there might be life experiences you need to have and work you need to do before a fulfilling purpose can click with you.

Perhaps being a parent offers you the kind of fulfillment that would fill that emptiness, but you wouldn't necessarily know that until after you have a child. Or maybe it's something more career-focused. Maybe your heart and mind are in tune with being on the sea, something you may not know until you set foot on a boat.

You may even feel a pull toward something that could offer you fulfillment, like a persistent interest or something that really speaks to you. That could help you find a direction.

2. Grief, The Death Of A Loved One

Grief is a natural emotional reaction to the death of a loved one. Sometimes we can see the end coming and have some time to mentally and emotionally prepare for it. Other times we may lose a loved one unexpectedly. There is always a flood of emotions to deal with when a death occurs, even if it's not immediate.

Many people turn to grief models to better try to process and understand their grief without really understanding the models. The "Five Stages of Grief" is one such model. What people tend to get wrong about these models is that they are not hard and fast rules. It's impossible to shove the full scope of emotions into such a narrow box, a fact that the creators of such models regularly talk about.

They may serve as a general guideline. There are stages that you may or may not experience. Some people experience multiple stages at the same time. Others bounce around through different stages as they are mourning their loved one.

Many of the models talk about "numbness" or "denial" as being involved in the grief process and this might explain the emptiness you feel. It can be a difficult experience because, rationally, you know that you should probably be feeling sadness along with lots of other emotions, but you don't and that's hard to reconcile.

Grief and mourning are more complicated than they appear. That makes it a good idea to seek a grief counselor. A grief specialist may be able to help you through those persistent empty feelings and mourning.

3. Drug And Alcohol Abuse

Many people turn to drugs and alcohol to cope with the traumas of their life. There's nothing inherently wrong with periodically having a drink or using legal substances. The problems really start to pick up when those substances are used excessively or as a way to help moderate one's emotions.

Filling the void of emptiness with a substance can lead to addiction, worse relationships with other people, losing jobs, and changing life circumstances.

Substance abuse can also lead to different physical or mental health issues, other than substance abuse disorder, like sparking a latent mental illness or liver disease. It may also make preexisting health issues worse.

Alcohol is known to impact people with mood disorders, like depression and bipolar disorder, far more severely than people without. It just works differently in their minds and may fuel emotional instability and make depression worse.

One of the reasons people use substances is to help them survive something they are going through. They believe it helps them because it calms them down at the moment. The problem is that extended substance use can have long-term effects that can worsen mental health issues or cause new ones to crop up in the future.

4. Long-Term Stresses

Humans aren't built to cope with long-term stresses well. Stress causes different hormones to be produced to help a person get through that immediate stressful situation, but those hormones can cause more significant problems the longer they are present.

Long-term stresses can cause depression, anxiety, and in some cases, PTSD. Survivors of domestic abuse, child abuse, and poverty may develop Complex PTSD, which results from never really getting a break from the circumstances they survived.

Avoiding long-term stresses or changing living situations may help. But if mental health problems have developed, it will require a trained mental health professional to heal and recover from.

Chapter 15:

Stop Giving a Damn About Everything

Our life is a series of decisions and the consequences of those decisions. But these decisions are not wholly of ours. They have been approved by many people, society, friends, family, and even the people we don't know. We care more about what people think about us than what makes us happy, and we are habitual of taking consent from others.

Have you ever thought about what privileges does it give you? Nothing! Except killing your self-esteem and making you insecure in public. Others grade our daily day-to-day choices to our career and job decisions.

You managed to impress them, but what good does it bring to you? It all leads to stress and anxiety stealing away your peace and leaving you in a constant struggle between your happiness and seeking approval.

Life settlements should be based on your desires and your definition of contentment. After all, it's your life, and you be the one living with the consequences.

You choose a job or a lifestyle that isn't what you craved for, and it's what your family wanted for you. And you are stuck with a 9 to 5 job you never wanted, and you are giving your hours and energy without an ounce of satisfaction.

You can't control everything in your life, but you can choose how to react to it. Everything that happens around you is not your headache, and what people might say about you is not something you should be bothered by.

Just like your business is not someone else's business, their business is not your business. The rule to a peaceful life is
"Mind your own business."
Someone bought a sports car, got fired, looked prettier than you, or was smiling all day. It would help if you were least concerned about all this. Nagging about someone's personal affairs might not affect them much, but it surely will destroy your tranquility.
Learn to be content in every situation. Develop an attitude of caring less. Is someone better than you? So what?
Did someone leave you? What's the big deal?

By acknowledging priorities in your life, you can stop giving a damn to people and everything. You can't just care about anything, and there has to be something specific. Align your ambitions and passions. Set your goals and fight your way towards them. You are going to meet a lot of people on your road who won't agree with you, but you are not here to impress them.

A happy person will criticize others less and will show more empathy. What someone opinions about you is his mindset. If you start listening to everyone on your road, do you think you'll ever make it to the end.? If you are going to stop and heed them? Then what about your motives and targets? Elements that you should be working on will lay neglected.

You have to be passionate about something in your life, a weighted purpose to stop caring about worthless things. And strive for it. Keeping your body and mind busy for a more significant cause makes you unaware of all the trivial matters.

As you progress in life, priorities tend to shift. You should know what holds the highest value and focus on those points that eventually lead to your happiness, give yourself more credit and appropriate your flaws.

Chapter 16:

Stop Overthinking

Thinking Optimally

Thinking is healthy for everybody. The fact that you do not think about anything is a red flag. Thinking gives you a range of choices in decision-making. You can evaluate one after another before settling for the best.

Good thinking is not a choice we have anyway. If you do not do it, somebody else will exploit you by thinking on your behalf. They may not act in good faith and you will be the victim.

Thinking is healthy and normal for any sane person. However, there are upper and lower limits in thinking. Retarded thinking will disable you from living or working optimally. Similarly, overthinking will deny you serenity in life.

Threshold Of Thoughts To Entertain

We should not every thought regardless of how enticing they are because their effects could be disastrous. We should sieve whatever we give attention to while allowing only the best to occupy our minds. However, do we have control over our thoughts?

Most people cannot take charge of their thoughts because they have not set their priorities right. Their minds cannot prioritize what is important because of their indecisiveness. They cannot let go of an idea or situation once they start pondering on it.

Overthinking is highly unrecompensed. Here are a few ways on how to stop it:

1. Accept Fate

Fate is unchallengeable. There is a different way to handle it if it is unfavorable. Living in denial will complicate matters instead of making them better. Be optimistic when doors shut in front of you. Consider it a way nature is warning you about the path you have chosen.

The universe naturally selects the best for us. Its blessings could come in unexpected ways. When we misjudge them for misfortunes, we will spend much time overthinking what we should have thanked the universe for.

Accepting fate is not giving up. It is stopping to overthink non-issues and moving on to more important ones. Overthinking is injurious to an uncertain future. We can bulldoze our way in things that we could have just left alone. Such mistakes are expensive to commit.

2. Count Your Blessings

One reason why people overthink is the fear of losing. It clouds their judgment to the extent of not remembering their past achievements. Think enough to get past a hurdle but do not prolong it further. Overthinking will not make problems go away. Instead, it could complicate them more.

Whenever you find yourself overthinking about something, retract your steps and be grateful for your achievements. Gratitude will open your eyes to the reality that you did not make it because of overthinking. Other factors were part of your success.

Overthinking will blind you from acknowledging your past victories. Fight it by reminding yourself that it had nothing to do with your success.

3.   Prioritize Your Health

A healthy lifestyle is worry-free. You can stop overthinking when you consider the status of your health. It does more harm than good. People with underlying health conditions like high blood pressure and diabetes are advised by doctors not to overthink for the sake of their health.

Overthinking could trigger ulcers. For the sake of good health, strive not to overthink trivial issues. Whenever you start overthinking, remember what it can do to your health. Prioritize your health above everything.

Consider the analogy of cigarette smokers and the health warning written boldly on the packets. If they could take the warning seriously, a majority of them would not fall to lung-related complications in old age. Similarly, there is a warning to stop overthinking in life lest you succumb to depression and anxiety.

In conclusion, it is paramount to stop overthinking because it changes nothing. Its demerits outweigh its benefits. It is a passive way of dealing with challenges. Instead of worrying about a problem, be proactive in seeking solutions.

When the burden of overthinking gets heavy, share it with your friends and you will find a solution together.

Chapter 17:

Meditate For Focus

Meditation calms the mind and helps you to focus on what is important. It dims the noise and brings your goals into clearer vision.

Meditation has been practiced as far back as 5000bc in India - with meditation depicted in wall artisan from that period.
That is 1500 years older than any written artefact ever found.
It is as old as the archaeological evidence of any human society.

Meditation can change the structure of the brain promoting focus, learning and better memory, as well as lowering stress and reducing the chances of anxiety and depression.

Whilst there are many different types and ways to meditate,
the ultimate goal is to clear your mind and calm your body
so that you can focus on your dream.
Aim to look inward for answers.
It could be aided by music relating to your dream or videos.
The music, the images, and imagining you are already living that life will bring it into reality.

Your mind creates the vision and the feeling

in your heart will bring it to you.

When your mind and heart work together it creates balance,

leading to happiness and success.

Meditation is the process of bringing the

visions of the mind and the desires of the heart together,

which in turn will form your life.

Meditation clears all the threats to this -

such as worry and distraction.

It will bring you clear focus and open up the next steps in your journey.

Meditation is often best done when you first wake or before you go to

sleep, but it can be incorporated into your day.

If clear consistent thought brings decisive action and success,

it is important to dwell on your dreams as often as possible.

Calm your mind of the unnecessary noise that is robbing you of your

focus.

The more realistic you make this vision

and the more you feel it in your heart,

the quicker it will come.

Meditation can help you achieve this

whether you follow a guide or make it up yourself.

The key is calm and focus.

Your subconscious knows how to get there.

Meditation will help open up that knowledge.

Science is just beginning to unlock the answers on why meditation is so effective, even so it has been used for over 7000 years to help people relax and focus on their goals.

The positive health and well-being evidence of meditation is well documented.

We may not yet understand it fully,

But just know that it works and use it every day.

You don't need to understand every detail to use something that works.

Meditation is perhaps one of the most time-tested tools in existence.

It could work for you, if you try it.

It could change your life forever.

Chapter 18:

Stop Ignoring Your Health

Do you have a busy life? Do you follow a hard and continuous regime of tasks every day for a significant amount of time? Have you ever felt that you cannot enjoy even the happiest moments of your life even if you want to? Let me highlight one reason you might recognize it straight away.

You are not enjoying your days while still being in all your senses because you don't have your mind and body in the right place.

All these years you have lived your life as a race. You have taken part in every event in and around your life just because you never wanted to miss anything. But in this process, you never lived your life to its full potential. You never lived a single moment with just the emotional intention of being then and there and not trying to live it like just another day or event.

People often get so busy with making their careers that they don't realize what is more important in life? It is their mental and physical health!

You will not get anywhere far in your life if you keep ignoring the signs of sickness your body keeps giving you. Your body is a machine with a conditional warranty. The day you violate the conditions of this warranty, life will become challenging, and you won't even be interested in the basic tasks at hand.

You might have heard the famous saying that "Health is Wealth". Let it sink in for a while and analyze your own life. You don't need to be a top-tier athlete to have a good body. You need a good body for your organs to work properly. You need an active lifestyle to be more productive and be more present and engaged in the things that are going around you.

The dilemma of our lives is that we don't care about what we have right now, but we care a lot about what we want. Not realizing that what we want might be cursed but what we have is the soul of good living. And that my friends are the blessing of health that most of us take for granted.

Most people have a tendency and devotion to work specifically on their health and fitness on a priority basis. They have a better standard of life. These people have a clearer mind to feel and capture the best moments in life with what their senses can offer best to them.

If you don't stop ignoring your health, you won't ever get out of this constant struggle. The struggle to find the reasons for you being detached from everything despite being involved every time.

Being careful and observant of your health doesn't make you selfish. This makes you a much more caring person because not only your life but the life of others around you is also affected by your sickness. Not only your resources are used for your treatments, but the attention and emotions of your loved ones are also being spent, just in hope of your wellness.

Chapter 19:

The Power of Breathing To Reset Your Mind

Breathing is something we often take for granted. The breath is always there where we notice or not, keeping us going, and keeping us alive. Without our breath, our hearts will not have enough oxygen and we will die a very agonizing death. Yet many of us forget to take the time out of the day to utilize this powerful tool of breathing mindfully to reset our focus, and to calm ourselves down in times of stress and anxiety.

Throughout the way, we are bombarded with things. Work stuff, people stuff, family stuff, and our minds and hearts begin racing and stay elevated throughout the day. Induced by stress hormones, we find ourselves full of cluttered thoughts and our productivity and focus drops as a result. Without clearing all these negative emotions that are bottled up inside us, we may find ourselves stressed out and unable to relax throughout the day, and even at night as we try to go to sleep.

This is where the power of conscious breathing comes into play. We all have the power and choice to take 30 seconds out of our day each time we feel that we need to settle down our emotions and clear our head.

Everytime you feel like things are getting out of control, simply stop whatever you are doing, close your eyes, and focus on breathing through our noise. Notice the breath that goes in and out of your nostrils as you inhale and exhale deeply.

By redirecting our focus to our breaths, we momentarily stop our automatic thoughts and are forced to direct attention to each intentional inhalation and exhalation. This conscious awareness to our breath serves to calm our nerves in times of volatility. If you don't believe it, try it for yourselves right now.

This technique has worked for me time and time again. Everytime I catch myself feeling distracted or unhappy, I would stop whatever I was doing, put on my noise cancelling earphones with the music turned off, and to just sit in complete silence as I focused on my breath. After about a minute or two, I find myself with a clearer head. A cleanse of sorts. And then i would attend to whatever task I was doing before.

This takes practice and awareness to be able to do consistently whenever negative emotions rise up. If you feel something is amiss 10x a day, you can carve out 10x of these deep breathing exercises each day as well. Try it and let me know your results.

Chapter 20:

How To Fight Worrying

The Good News

The good news in town is that you should stop worrying. Worry is a feeling of anxiety that stems from fear of failure. Our success is contributed by some factors that we may not have control over. It is unfair for us to judge ourselves harshly based on them.

Worrying will not change anything. We should focus on how we can change the situation instead of worrying about it. We try to meet the expectations that people have of us. The fear of letting them down is a cause of worry.

The Genesis Of Worrying

Worrying is caused by many other factors apart from the expectations of other people on us. We are afraid of letting ourselves down. Our history of failure could haunt us and we become uncertain whether we can change it.

Another cause of worry is the fear of the consequences of non-performance. We are afraid of what may befall us when we fail to succeed.

The genesis of constant worry could also come from childhood trauma. Experiences as children shape our adulthood. There could be no valid reason for us to worry but past experiences can make us always anxious. All reasons for worrying are valid. It is a natural human feeling but we should not allow it to overtake our mental stability.

Stop Worrying

There could be many reasons why you should worry but there are twice as much why you should not. Although worrying is a subconscious emotion that we hardly have control over, we can address the potential sources of worry.

Here is how to:

1. Do Not Be A People-Pleaser

You cannot stop people from having expectations from you on anything. They can have their opinion about your ability and there is nothing you can do about it. However, do not live trying to impress them. You owe them nothing.

Continue pursuing your dreams without gauging yourself against their expectations. You will not strain and wear yourself out as you seek their approval. Prioritize your ambitions above their expectations and you will have nothing to worry about.

2. Be Self-Confident

Believe in yourself even when others doubt you. You will not worry about failure when you are self-confident. The greatest gift to yourself is trusting in your ability to deliver on your mandate. Do not worry about what you cannot control.

Worrying will pressure you to act wrongly. Delayed right action is better than a fast wrong move. Have the mental strength to withstand external pressure and believe in yourself.

3. Face Your Fears

Past trauma could indeed have a long-lasting impact on our adulthood. Our worry could be because of childhood abuse. We were punished when we could not perform and consequently developed performance anxiety.

Stop worrying because that ugly phase has passed. Fight performance anxiety by doing your best. Repeat what you were unable to do in childhood and succeed. You will no longer worry about it in the future.

4. Make A Move

If you can change something, why worry? Still, why worry if you cannot change it? This is a call to action. Worrying alone will change nothing. Do not despise your position. Make a bold move that you see can make things better.

Responsible adulting is proactive. Act without waiting on instructions. Your actions are for the greater good. There could be other people who have the same worry as you. It is a blessing when you make a move and assure them not to worry.

5. Look At The Brighter Side

Learn to look at the good side in every situation. There could be a reason why things are not moving as you expect. Your worry could be a deliberate act of nature for the greater good.

Looking at the brighter side will make you not worry about a lot of things. In due time, everything will work out as planned.

In conclusion, fighting worry is a deliberate decision that we make. Except we do it, no one will do it for you. These five ways will lead you out of worry.

Chapter 21:

How Going Outside More Can Make You Happy

Do you ever find yourself feeling calmer, more relaxed, or more focused after spending time in nature? That's because time outside has studied and proven benefits for your mental health. Mental illness affects one in five humans in any given year. Let's talk about what some Vitamin N (nature) can do for your mental health…

A simple stay in the outdoors can do wonders for relieving anxiety, stress, and depression. Countless studies have proven that nature has a positive effect on your mental health. What you see, hear, and experience in nature can improve your mood in a moment.

There is a strong connection between time spent in nature and reduced negative emotions. This includes symptoms of anxiety, depression, and psychosomatic illnesses like irritability, insomnia, tension headaches, and indigestion. Feeling stressed? Research shows a link between exposure to nature and stress reduction. Stress is relieved within minutes of exposure to nature as measured by muscle tension, blood pressure, and brain activity. Time in green spaces significantly reduces your cortisol, which is a stress hormone. Nature also boosts endorphin levels and dopamine production, which promotes happiness.

Nature has a myriad of other brain benefits as well. Contact with nature has restorative properties, increasing energy and improving feelings of vitality and focus. Being nearby to nature has been shown to reduce symptoms of ADHD. Are you stuck on a project or idea? Being outside also improves creative thinking. Proximity to green space can restore capacity for concentration and attention.

Trouble sleeping? A two-hour walk in the woods is enough to improve sleep quality and help relieve sleep problems. Sleeping away from artificial light and waking up with natural sunlight can reset your circadian rhythm, which will help you feel refreshed after a better night's sleep.

Nature can also help with the grief process. This is because exposure to nature causes better coping, including improved self-awareness, self-concept, and positively affected mood. The positive effects of nature affect the way you treat others. People are more caring and positive when they are exposed to and around various forms of nature.

Getting outdoors doesn't have to be a lot of work. There are lots of simple ways you can get quality time in nature. Start with taking a walk in the woods. Nature walks help combat stress while improving mental well-being. Want to take your walk to the next level? Try forest bathing.

Move your workout into the outdoors. Regular use of natural areas for physical activity can reduce the risk of mental health problems by 50%.

Completing activities like walking, cycling, jogging, or doing yoga in a natural environment makes you happier than in the city

Engage your senses to maximize the health benefits of being outside. Breathe deep, as the scent of fresh pine has been shown to lower stress and anxiety. Make sure to pause and listen, as studies show that listening to nature sounds like bird songs and rushing water can help lower stress levels. Book a camping trip. Immersing yourself in nature for a longer period of time is the best way to absorb the health benefits of the outdoors.

Chapter 22:

Living in the Moment

Today we're going to talk about a topic that will help those of you struggling with fears and anxieties about your past and even about your future. And I hope that at the end of this video, you may be able to live a life that is truly more present and full.

So, what is living in the moment all about and why should we even bother?

You see, for many of us, since we're young, we've been told to plan for our future. And we always feel like we're never enough until we achieve the next best grade in class, get into a great university, get a high paying career, and then retire comfortably. We always look at our life as an endless competition, and that we believe that there will always be more time to have fun and enjoy life later when we have worked our asses off and clawed our way to success. Measures that are either set by our parents, society, or our peers. And this constant desire to look ahead, while is a good motivator if done in moderation and not obsessively, can lead us to always being unhappy in our current present moment.

Because we are always chasing something bigger, the goal post keeps moving farther and farther away every time we reach one. And the reality is that we will never ever be happy with ourselves at any point if that becomes our motto. We try to look so far ahead all the time that we miss the beautiful sights along the way. We miss the whole point of our goals which is not to want the end goal so eagerly, but to actually enjoy the process, enjoy the journey, and enjoy each step along the way. The struggles, the sadness, the accomplishments, the joy. When we stop checking out the flowers around us, and when we stop looking around the beautiful sights, the destination becomes less amazing.

Reminding ourselves to live in the present helps us keep things in perspective that yes, even though our ultimate dream is to be this and that career wise, or whatever it may be, that we must not forget that life is precious, and that each day is a blessing and that we should cherish each living day as if it were your last.

Forget the idea that you might have 30 years to work before you can tell ur self that you can finally relax and retire. Because you never know if you will even have tomorrow. If you are always reminded that life is fragile and that your life isn't always guaranteed, that you become more aware that you need to live in the moment in order to live your best life. Rid yourself of any worries, anxieties, and fears you have about the future because the time will come when it comes. Things will happen for you eventually so long as you do what you need to do each and every day without obsessing over it.

Sometimes our past failures and shortcomings in the workplace can have an adverse effect on how we view the present as well. And this cycle perpetuates itself over and over again and we lose sight of what's really important to us. Our family, our friends, our pets, and we neglect them or neglect to spend enough time with them thinking we have so much time left. But we fail to remember again that life does not always work the way we want it to. And we need to be careful not to fall into that trap that we have complete and total control over our life and how our plans would work out.

In the next video we will talk about how to live in the moment if you have anxieties and fears about things unrelated to work. Whether it be a family issue or a health issue. I want to address that in a separate topic.

Chapter 23:

7 Steps for Health Anxiety Recovery

Even when you're healthy, that controlled worry about your health is normal. However, if such concerns become uncontrollable, you may have developed health anxiety. Health anxiety can affect anyone, whether they are healthy or have an existing health condition. In extreme cases, health anxiety will cause you a great deal of distress and, however, adversely affect your daily life or things you love and your relationships. The plain fact about health anxiety is that it causes an irrational fear of severe health conditions. As a result, any physical symptoms, even normal bodily functions, frequently cause health concerns. A burn or pimple on your body. Could it be Skin cancer? Sweating at night. Could it be HIV or lymphoma? Headaches? You already know it isn't a brain tumor! You might well be having a lot of negative or scary ideas right now. However, every situation is backed with ample remedies or mitigations.

Here are 7 steps for health anxiety recovery.

1. Learn More About Anxiety

The first step toward recovery is to acquire every bit of information relating to anxiety in general. That is, studying the physiology of the body's reaction to anxiety triggers. You'll discover that in most anxiety cases, such bodily reactions are typically caused by relatively harmless circumstances. It is, therefore, essential that you learn ways that will promote control over such reactions.

2. Seek Cognitive-Behaviour Therapy

CBT is a type of therapy that focuses on your cognition, how you think, and your behaviours. It is rooted from the notion that the type of emotions you feel whenever you are facing a certain situation influences how you respond and behave. CBT involves altering the patterns of your thinking and opinions that cause anxiety and coaching you to confront your fears to desensitize you. It enables you to train yourself to approach the fear factor that triggers anxiety.

3.   Shift Your Focus

A person who suffers from health anxiety usually concentrates more on how the body functions. The more you concentrate on how your body functions, the more you'll notice physical sensations. As a result, you're most likely to develop worrying thoughts of physical symptoms. In such cases, divert your attention to something else to distract yourself from the troubling thoughts.

4.   Exercise Mindfulness

Practicing mindfulness is the art of feeling your present self, that is being in the moment and allowing your body to feel the situation as it is. It further entails paying attention to the present moment and disconnecting from unhelpful thoughts. While the practice has its roots in meditation, it has found increasing use in therapy. Mindfulness-based cognitive and behavioural is highly effective for people suffering from health anxiety.

5.   Avoid Google-Searching Your Symptoms

If you already have health anxiety, Google is not your friend. Avoid using Google to look up the causes of what you physically feel because this will only make your worries worse. A distressing thought is a channel for imagining the worst-case scenarios. You must maintain a balanced perspective on your situation.

6. Practice Cognitive Diffusion

Thoughts are only perceptions and should not be used to establish your reality. When you ruminate, you start to believe that your thoughts reflect your reality. For instance, a person with health anxiety who often worries about their heart may think they have a heart condition when a physical symptom arises. When you practice cognitive diffusion, you can identify and challenge your negative thought, allowing you to reframe them.

7. Work With What Works for You

It's normal to feel overwhelmed when you try out a technique that has been successful to several people, and it turns out to be conflicting. It unsurprising that not every remedy is relevant for everyone experiencing health anxiety disorder. This is because each person is affected differently. You'll want to find what works best for your specific case, which may necessitate a few trials and errors.

Conclusion

Like other anxiety disorders, health anxiety can be daunting to your whole existence. You find yourself constantly worrying about getting sick or falling ill. You frequently get concerned about any physical symptoms you are experiencing and what they may mean. If health-related feelings, concerns, and thoughts begin to dominate your daily life, it may be time to take action.

Chapter 24:

7 Signs of Social Anxiety

It is a well-known fact that the times we're living in today are fraught with unprecedented anxiety. But eventually we find ways to bounce back like nothing happened. Even so, there are certain anxious patterns in your life that you might need extra help to break. If you feel overly uncomfortable, or stressed with the mere thought of social situations that you avoid social gatherings at all costs, you might have social anxiety disorder.

Social anxiety according to mayo clinic is a "social phobia," or fear that causes avoidance of social events or situations in fear of being judged by others. It is based on the notion that you might do or say something within the context of social interactions and end up embarrassing or humiliating yourself. On that account, you develop a deep and sometimes irrational fear of being judged or rejected by others.

Here are 7 signs of social anxiety.

1. You've Had This Feeling Ever Since You Were A Teen

The Diagnostic and Statistical Manuals define social anxiety disorder as a time limit. You must have felt this way for six months to be eligible. However, scientists have discovered that the average age at which social anxiety manifests itself is around 13, with most cases occurring between the ages of 11 and 19. This is the period when you're most self-conscious because your adolescent brains are usually more sensitive to other people's reactions. It's pretty uncommon for a social anxiety disorder to manifest after 25, so you might be okay if you've made it that far.

2. You're Overly Sensitive to Criticism

Being criticized doesn't settle well for anyone, and it is incredibly distressing when you have a social anxiety disorder. That's because what you always dread is coming true. Since you are constantly worried about being rejected or judged by others, social anxiety makes you overly sensitive to everything critical, criticizing, or ridiculing. It even prevents you from seizing a possible opportunity because you're constantly looking for failure or humiliation.

3. Self-Esteem Issues

It is common knowledge that many nervous disorders are correlated to self-esteem issues, and social anxiety is not exempt. Studies show that many psychological disorders such as body image issues, fear, and frustration are closely linked to this disorder. The greater your social anxiety, the lower your self-esteem.

4. You Are Self-Conscious

Recent studies show that highly impaired people with social anxiety lack strong social networks. As Thomas Rodebaugh, puts it, "social anxiety makes you think you are coming across much worse than you are." They are always self-conscious and miscalculating how badly they appear in relationships or friendships and might even pass up a job opportunity in fear of being rejected or singled out as a failure.

5. Extreme Physical Symptoms of Anxiety

Social anxiety disorder manifests itself in your thoughts and your body. Panic attacks and anxiety become severe and frequent when you encounter a social situation or do something you regret. The Mayo Clinic lists the physical symptoms to include: Sweating, shortness of breath, muscle tension, fast heart rate, a desire to run, dizziness, nausea, and becoming blank. The symptoms are typically your body's response to fear or a genuine upsetting feeling.

6. You Turn to Substance Abuse for Normal Functionality

Research has proven a high correlation between alcohol or drug misuse and social phobia. The severity of social phobia can sometimes reach a point where sufferers resort to substance abuse. That is, you need drugs to feel comfortable or function properly. If you're always in dire need of drinking or smoking a joint before any social event and feeling guilty later, it's a sign.

7. You Fear Asking Anything in Public

When you're a person who suffers a lot in public, this is a sentimental sign that you could be suffering from a social anxiety. Of course, people with social anxiety disorder are hesitant to ask for simple things, such as food or just anything in public places. Even in places where no one knows you, you still feel this way.

Conclusion

It is okay to feel shy or thrilled before or during a social event. However, if the thought of being social or being in a social setting creates terror within you, something is wrong. You might consider seeking help.

Chapter 25:

Don't Stay At Home

Today we're going to talk about why you should consider getting out of your house as much as possible, especially if you need to get work done, or if you have some other important personal projects that requires your undivided attention to complete.

For those that work full-time jobs, we all aspire to one day be able to work from home. We all dream of one day being able to just get up from our beds and walk over to our desks to begin work.

Having tried this myself for the last 4 years, I can safely tell you that staying at home isn't all that amazing as it has been talked up or hyped up to be.

While it may sound nice to be able to work from home, in reality, distractions are tough to avoid, and procrastination is one major killer of productivity at home. Many of us have made our homes the Center of entertainment and relaxation. We buy nice couches, TVs, beds, speakers, etc., and all these items around the house are temptations for us to slack off.

For those who are living with family, or who have pets, their presence could also disrupt our productivity.

Without people around us to motivate us to keep working hard, we tend to just tell ourselves "it's okay I'll just watch this one show and then I'll get back to work", and before we know it, it is 5pm and we haven't done a single thing.

Some people love it, some people hate it, but personally, I much prefer getting my butt out of the house and into a co-working space, a cafe, or a library, where I can visually see other people working hard, which motivates me to stay away from slacking off.

Having been doing regular journaling to measure my productivity, staying at home has always resulted in my worst daily performance no matter how hard I try to make my home environment the most conducive for work. Feeling like taking nap because my bed is right there, or watching a Netflix show on my big screen tv, has always been hard to resist. You will be surprised how many hours you are potentially losing from just indulging in any of these things.

For those who really has no choice but to work from home, either to save money, or because you need to take care of a family member. I would highly suggest that you optimize your environment to give yourself the greatest chance of success.

Dedicate a room that will be made into your study/work room, ensure that there is adequate and bright lighting, and to Keep all possible distractions outside the room. Putting your work desk in your bedroom is the worst thing you can do because you will blur the lines between rest and work if you mix the two things up in one tiny space. Not only will you feel sluggish working from your bedroom, but you might also develop sleep issues as well.

Not staying at home is still your best bet for success. Find a space outside where you can be focused and have the discipline to get yourself there every single day, no matter how tired or lethargic you feel. Once you leave the house, you have already won half the battle in getting your productivity under control.

Chapter 26:

How to Face Difficulties in Life

Have you noticed that difficulties in life come in gangs attacking you when you're least prepared for them? The effect is like being forced to endure an unrelenting nuclear attack.

Overcoming obstacles in life is hard. But life is full of personal challenges, and we have to summon the courage to face them. These test our emotional mettle — injury, illness, unemployment, grief, divorce, death, or even a new venture with an unknown future. Here are some strategies to help carry you through:

1. Turn Toward Reality

So often, we turn away from life rather than toward it. We are masters of avoidance! But if we want to be present—to enjoy life and be more effective in it—we must orient ourselves toward facing reality. When guided by the reality principle, we develop a deeper capacity to deal with life more effectively. What once was difficult is now easier. What once frightened us now feels familiar. Life becomes more manageable. And there's something even deeper that we gain: Because we can see that we have grown stronger, we have greater confidence that we can grow even stronger still. This is the basis of feeling capable, which is the wellspring of a satisfying life.

2. Embrace Your Life as It Is Rather Than as You Wish It to Be

The Buddha taught that the secret to life is to want what you have and do not want what you don't have. Being present means being present to the life that you have right here, right now. There is freedom in taking life as it comes to us—the good with the bad, the wonderful with the tragic, the love with the loss, and the life with the death. When we embrace it all, then we have a real chance to enjoy life, value our experiences, and mine the treasures that are there for the taking. When we surrender to the reality of who we are, we give ourselves a chance to do what we can do.

3. Take Your Time

As the story of the tortoise and the hare tells us, slow and steady wins the race. By being in a hurry, we actually thwart our own success. We get ahead of ourselves. We make more mistakes. We cut corners and pay for them later. We may learn the easy way but not necessarily the best way. As an old adage puts it: The slower you go, the sooner you get there.

Slow, disciplined, incremental growth is the kind of approach that leads to lasting change.

Chapter 27:

How To Focus on Creating Positive Actions

Only a positive person can lead a healthy life. Imagine waking up every day feeling like you are ready to face the day's challenges and you are filled with hope about life. That is something an optimist doesn't have to imagine because they already feel it every day. Also, scientifically, it is proven that optimistic people have a lower chance of dying because of a stress-caused disease. Although positive thinking will not magically vanish all your problems, it will make them seem more manageable and somewhat not a big deal.

Positive thinking is what leads to positive actions, actions that affect you and the people around you. When you think positively, your actions show how positive you are. You can create positive thinking by focusing on the good in life, even if it may feel tiny thing to feel happy about because when you once learn to be satisfied with minor things, you would think that you no longer feel the same amount of stress as before and now you would feel freer. This positive attitude will always find the good in everything, and life would seem much easier than before.

Being grateful for the things you have contributed a lot to your positive behavior. Gratitude has proven to reduce stress and improve self-esteem. Think of the things you are grateful for; for example, if someone gives you good advice, then be thankful to them, for if someone has helped you with something, then be grateful to them, by being grateful about minor things, you feel more optimistic about life, you feel that good things have always been coming to you. Studies show that making down a list of things you are grateful for during hard days helps you survive through the tough times.

A person laughing always looks like a happy person. Studies have shown that laughter lowers stress, anxiety, and depression. Open yourself up to humor, permit yourself to laugh even if forced because even a forced laugh can improve your mood. Laughter lightens the mood and makes problems seem more manageable. Your laughter is contagious, and it may even enhance the perspective of the people around us.

People with depression or anxiety are always their jailers; being harsh on themselves will only cause pain, negativity, and insecurity. So try to be soft with yourself, give yourself a positive talk regularly; it has proven to affect a person's actions. A positive word to yourself can influence your ability to regulate your feelings and thoughts. The positivity you carry in your brain is expressed through your actions, and who doesn't loves an optimistic person. Instead of blaming yourself, you can think differently, like "I will do better next time" or "I can fix this." Being optimistic about the complicated situation can lead your brain to find a solution to that problem.

When you wake up, it is good to do something positive in the morning, which mentally freshens you up. You can start the day by reading a positive quote about life and understand the meaning of that quote, and you may feel an overwhelming feeling after letting the meaning set. Everybody loves a good song, so start by listening to a piece of music that gives you positive vibes, that gives you hope, and motivation for the day. You can also share your positivity by being nice to someone or doing something nice for someone; you will find that you feel thrilled and positive by making someone else happy.

Surely you can't just start thinking positively in a night, but you can learn to approach things and people with a positive outlook with some practice.

Chapter 28:

It's Okay To Feel Uncertain

We are surrounded by a world that has endless possibilities. A world where no two incidents can predict the other. A realm where we are a slave to the unpredictable future and its repercussions.

Everyone has things weighing on their mind. Some of us know it and some of us keep carrying these weights unknowingly.

The uncertainty of life is the best gift that you never wanted. But when you come to realize the opportunities that lie at every uneven corner are worth living for.

Life changes fast, sometimes in our favor and sometimes not much. But life always has a way to balance things out. We only need to find the right approach to make things easier for us and the ones around us.

Everyone gets tested once in a while, but we need to find ways to cope with life when things get messy.

The worst thing the uncertainty of life can produce is the fear in your heart. The fear to never know what to expect next. But you can never let fear rule you.

To worry about the future ahead of us is pointless. So change the question from 'What if?' to 'What will I do if.'

If you already have this question popping up in your brain, this means that you are already getting the steam off.

You don't need to fear the uncertain because you can never wreck your life in any such direction from where there is no way back.

The uncertainty of life is always a transformation period to make you realize your true path. These uncertainties make you realize the faults you might have in your approach to things.

You don't need to worry about anything unpredictable and unexpected because not everything is out of your control every time. Things might not happen in a way you anticipated but that doesn't mean you cannot be prepared for it.

There are a lot of things that are in your control and you are well researched and well equipped to go around events. So use your experience to do the damage control.

Let's say you have a pandemic at your hand which you couldn't possibly predict, but that doesn't mean you cannot do anything to work on its effects. You can raise funds for the affected population. You can try to find new ways to minimize unemployment. You can find alternate ways to keep the economy running and so on.

Deal with your emotions as you cannot get carried away with such events being driven by your feelings.

Don't avoid your responsibilities and don't delay anything. You have to fulfill every task expected of you because you were destined to do it. The results are not predetermined on a slate but you can always hope for the best be the best version of yourself no matter how bad things get.

Life provides us with endless possibilities because when nothing is certain, anything is possible. So be your own limit.

Chapter 29:

Putting Exercise First

In this topic we're going to talk about why you should consider putting exercise first above all else in your daily routine and the benefits that it can bring to your health and all other aspects of your life.

Many of us don't usually prioritise work as the most essential part of our day. We have work, family, kids, money, and a whole host of problems to worry about that exercise usually comes in dead last on the list of things to do. What we fail to realise is that exercise is the one thing that we might need most to keep us fit and healthy to take on the challenges that life throws at us each and every day.

I'm sure you all know the benefits of exercise. Doing it regularly can bring lots of benefits to your metabolism, alertness, energy, BMI, muscle mass, and so on. But what does it really mean?

Have you ever wondered why you are always feeling tired all the time? Or why you feel like you haven't really woken up yet when you're already sitting in front of your desk at the office?

You see, it is the time of your exercise that matters a lot too. A lot of successful CEOs and entrepreneurs actually make exercise the first thing they do when they wake up from bed. The reason is simple, it gets the body moving which in turns starts the engine that drives you out of lethargy and into an active physical state. As you move on a treadmill or do yoga early in the morning, your heart starts pumping faster which drives more blood into other areas of your body to wake you up.

And this sets you up for success because you are no longer in a state of slumber and sluggishness. Exercising first thing in the morning also has the added benefit of checking it off your list early so that you do not wait for the lazy bug to tell you not to enter the gym.

Sure getting up earlier to exercise might also be a struggle in of itself, but you do not necessarily have to travel to a gym far away to get your daily exercise. Simply stepping out of the house for a quick run or finding an empty space in your house where you will not be disturbed and begin a yoga routine that you can find on YouTube will also suffice. As long as you get the body moving and in a state of flow, you would have already won the day.

Putting exercise first above all else in your day also gives you a sense of accomplishment that you have taken the action to improve your health consistently. Losing excess body fat will also increase your energy levels and help you get through the challenges of your work day with greater ease.

If you find that exercising first thing in the morning is just impossible to do for some reason, make it a point to schedule it sometime before midday, preferably during your lunch break. Leaving exercise to the night will only trigger more excuses from your brain not to go as your will power gets depleted more and more throughout the day. From experience, unless I have booked a class that i can't back out of in the evening, more often than not I will find many more excuses not to go than if I had scheduled exercise early in the day.

If there is a sport that you particularly like, I also urge you to schedule more games with friends or family throughout the week as you are more likely to show up for them seeing that you already favour the sport over other exercises. In my case I love tennis and would almost never miss a session that I have scheduled. Gym and yoga on the other hand, I am more inclined to give it a miss if given the opportunity.

So, for those of you who want to operate in a higher state of mind, body, and spirit, I challenge you to make exercise your number one priority and put it at the top of your list of things to do for the day. You will find your mind will be clearer and you will know exactly what you need to do for the day as you flow with the exercise. Feel free to play your favourite music playlist as you work out as well.

Chapter 30:

Renewing Your Mind

The Diversity Of The Mind

The mind is an invisible part of the human body yet very vital in determining the direction and quality of life. It is what distinguishes the different types of people. Moreover, the mind is an equalizer that unites people at the same table because they share ideologies.

Differences of opinions and ideologies borne by the mind have segregated people into different classes. Those believing in a particular cause pursue it because they are convinced it is the right way while those holding alternative views associate with the like-minded. Only time proves a thought right or wrong.

The Mind Is A Source Of Hope

The mind is responsible for a lot of innovations. The world owes it some of its life-changing innovations. It is a source of hope, how much so when renewed?

All innovations sprout from sober minds and have given much hope to humanity. There were very many people at the time yet only a handful were capable of solving problems like over-reliance on daylight and swift transport from one point to another.

A renewed mind is a tool to combat ignorance and poverty. It sets one on edge in living large and attaining their set goals. Moreover, it gives us a better perspective on how we can be victorious.

The path to renewing the mind is less traveled because it involves a lot of sacrifices. Here are proven ways on how to renew your mind:

1. Subscribe To A Higher Calling

There is an authority above us unto which we need to submit to. Like the food chain, there is always someone higher than you. It could be a philanthropist, religious leader, scholar, or someone you look up to for inspiration.

A role model in your life inspires you to think in a particular fashion. You will want to adopt their philosophies and align yourself with their beliefs. Slowly, you will be inducted into their different approaches to life.

Set your heart upon heeding to doctrines from an authority like religion. It will teach you how to turn from your old ways to new ones that are fit for believers. Your mind will be transformed to grasp new teachings.

You will work towards fulfilling certain expectations in the religion you ascribe to. Fellowshipping with those you share a belief reinforces your new school of thought.

2. Practice New Ways

The mind is like a muscle. It gets stronger as you exercise it. We get stuck in past ideologies, beliefs, and practices even when we are in a new era. It is natural to be hesitant to try out new things but we need to conquer our fears and be open to change.

Be proactive to try new things and your mind will register new experiences. They may change your initial stance on many issues. You will realize that the food you detest so much is not bad after all, your harshest critics could be your genuine fans, or the company you shun could be where you belong.

Your mind embraces change when you continually practice new ways. It is renewed and re-birthed into a new life. In new practices, the mind is trained to adapt to them and the thinking pattern is renewed. A monotonous lifestyle makes the mind get used to only one routine. It is hardly renewed.

3. Accept Correction

Correction is an integral part of learning. We are not always right and sometimes we need to be shown the right way. The mind can learn new skills and be rebuked when wrong. Nobody has a monopoly of knowledge.

A renewed mind accepts correction whenever it has strayed without which its doom is imminent. Let go of fallacies, unlearn misconceptions and learn facts.

In conclusion, renewing the mind is tedious if you do not observe the three ways discussed herein. Commit yourself to it and watch the transformation.

Chapter 31:

Stop Ignoring Your Health

Do you have a busy life? Do you follow a hard and continuous regime of tasks every day for a significant amount of time? Have you ever felt that you cannot enjoy even the happiest moments of your life even if you want to? Let me highlight one reason you might recognize it straight away.

You are not enjoying your days while still being in all your senses because you don't have your mind and body in the right place.

All these years you have lived your life as a race. You have taken part in every event in and around your life just because you never wanted to miss anything. But in this process, you never lived your life to its full potential. You never lived a single moment with just the emotional intention of being then and there and not trying to live it like just another day or event.

People often get so busy with making their careers that they don't realize what is more important in life? It is their mental and physical health!

You will not get anywhere far in your life if you keep ignoring the signs of sickness your body keeps giving you. Your body is a machine with a conditional warranty. The day you violate the conditions of this warranty, life will become challenging, and you won't even be interested in the basic tasks at hand.

You might have heard the famous saying that "Health is Wealth". Let it sink in for a while and analyze your own life. You don't need to be a top-tier athlete to have a good body. You need a good body for your organs to work properly. You need an active lifestyle to be more productive and be more present and engaged in the things that are going around you.

The dilemma of our lives is that we don't care about what we have right now, but we care a lot about what we want. Not realizing that what we want might be cursed but what we have is the soul of good living. And that my friends are the blessing of health that most of us take for granted.

Most people have a tendency and devotion to work specifically on their health and fitness on a priority basis. They have a better standard of life. These people have a clearer mind to feel and capture the best moments in life with what their senses can offer best to them.

If you don't stop ignoring your health, you won't ever get out of this constant struggle. The struggle to find the reasons for you being detached from everything despite being involved every time.

Being careful and observant of your health doesn't make you selfish. This makes you a much more caring person because not only your life but the life of others around you is also affected by your sickness. Not only your resources are used for your treatments, but the attention and emotions of your loved ones are also being spent, just in hope of your wellness.